Heaven
Is a Wonderful
Place

Angela M. Burrin
Illustrated by Gustavo Mazali

MW00947023

Abigail and Michael are twins. They have just finished second grade and are spending part of their summer vacation with Grandma Nancy. All week they've been asking her lots of questions. Abigail wanted to know how Grandma made her favorite cookies. And when they were at the zoo, Michael asked, "How do giraffes sleep?"

One rainy afternoon they said to her, "Grandma, we know Grandpa is in heaven. But what's heaven like? What is Grandpa doing there?"

"I've never seen heaven," said Grandma, "so I can't say for sure what it's like. But I can give you some really good clues from the Bible and from what our Catholic

faith teaches us. I looked them up when your grandpa died."

Grandma Nancy picked up her Bible from the coffee table. "Come sit next to me here on the sofa, and together we'll take a journey through the Bible."

"That's going to be fun," said Michael.

Abigail laughed, "A journey through the Bible with our favorite Grandma Nancy!"

Grandma Nancy opened her Bible.

"Abigail and Michael, just like you, Jesus' disciples liked to ask questions. One day they asked, 'Jesus, how do we pray?' Jesus answered, 'When you pray, say 'Our Father, who art in heaven.'

"So that's the first clue. Heaven is the place where your heavenly Father lives. He's your Father, and Jesus'

Father, and mine too. He's our Father, and we are all
part of God's family."

Grandma paused for a moment. "And did you know
that in heaven, people can do something we can't do?
They can see their heavenly Father's kind and loving
face."

Michael liked this clue. "Oh, I hope Grandpa is
looking at him right now!"

Grandma Nancy opened her Bible to another page.

"Are you ready for another clue?" she asked. "This one is about Jesus. When he was on earth, he taught people about his Father, and he healed many who were sick. He even raised people from the dead! Then Jesus died on the cross for our sins."

Michael chimed in, "And rose from the dead three days later!"

Grandma said, "That's right, Michael. And do you know what happened then? Forty days after his resurrection, Jesus went to the top of a mountain. The disciples were with him. They watched as he ascended into heaven. Now Jesus is in heaven ready to welcome us."

"Michael, I wonder what people do when they meet Jesus in heaven for the first time," Abigail said.

"I know what I'll do," said Michael. "I'll give Jesus a big hug!"

9

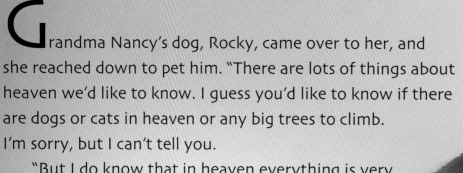

Grandma Nancy's dog, Rocky, came over to her, and she reached down to pet him. "There are lots of things about heaven we'd like to know. I guess you'd like to know if there are dogs or cats in heaven or any big trees to climb. I'm sorry, but I can't tell you.

"But I do know that in heaven everything is very bright! Here's the clue: one day Jesus showed his heavenly glory to his disciples, Peter, James, and John, on the top of a mountain. We say he was transfigured. Jesus' clothes suddenly became dazzlingly white, and his face shone like the sun.

"Now that Jesus is in heaven, he is just as radiant as on that day. And so everything around him shines brightly. I like to think that even the colors of the flowers and the wings of the angels glow!"

Michael laughed. "I wonder if everyone has to wear sunglasses!"

Grandma Nancy was quiet for a moment, and then she asked, "Who has a question for me?"

"Where do people live in heaven?" Abigail asked.

"I found a clue about that too," Grandma said. "Jesus told his disciples, 'In my Father's house there are many rooms.' Then he promised that he was going to prepare a place for them. What do you think your room will look like?"

"I want my room to be purple and pink," said Abigail.

"I'd like a really big chair in mine," said Michael.

Grandma smiled. "And I have another clue for you about what it's like to live in heaven," she said. "The Bible says that the gates in heaven are made of pearls and the streets are paved with gold. Imagine stepping out of your room onto glistening, gleaming sidewalks!"

Michael's mouth dropped open. "Streets of gold. I wonder if Grandpa has walked on them!"

Grandma Nancy gave Abigail and Michael a hug and said, "This clue will make you both happy. In heaven everyone is healthy. No one has upset stomachs or headaches. No one has cancer or any other disease. No one uses crutches or wheelchairs. No one will ever die.

"And imagine this: in heaven, no one cries, has a tantrum, or fights. Everyone gets along with everyone else. Doesn't heaven sound like a wonderful place?"

"But I miss Grandpa and all the fun things we did together," said Michael.

"And I still cry sometimes when I think about him," said Abigail.

"I know," said Grandma. "I miss him too. That's why it makes me feel better to think about heaven and what Grandpa might be doing there."

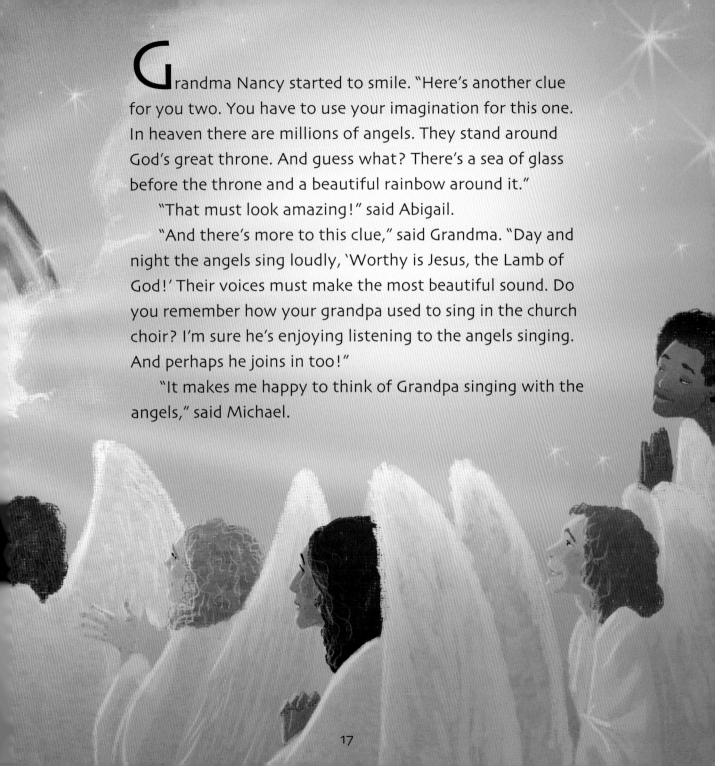

Grandma Nancy started to smile. "Here's another clue for you two. You have to use your imagination for this one. In heaven there are millions of angels. They stand around God's great throne. And guess what? There's a sea of glass before the throne and a beautiful rainbow around it."

"That must look amazing!" said Abigail.

"And there's more to this clue," said Grandma. "Day and night the angels sing loudly, 'Worthy is Jesus, the Lamb of God!' Their voices must make the most beautiful sound. Do you remember how your grandpa used to sing in the church choir? I'm sure he's enjoying listening to the angels singing. And perhaps he joins in too!"

"It makes me happy to think of Grandpa singing with the angels," said Michael.

17

Grandma Nancy took the lid off her cookie jar.

"My next clue is about something else people do in heaven. Can you guess? They cheer every time one person on earth chooses to stop doing what is wrong and turns to Jesus. They even have a party!"

Abigail asked, "A party? Why?"

Grandma explained, "Jesus told a story about a good shepherd who left ninety-nine

18

sheep to look for the one who was lost. And he said that all of heaven rejoices when even one sinner says he's sorry."

Michael finished his cookie and said, "I bet Grandpa cheers when I say, 'Jesus I'm sorry.'"

"Jesus loves you so much, Michael," said Grandma. "And it makes Jesus so happy when all of us stay close to him."

Grandma Nancy flipped through the pages of her Bible again.

"Abigail and Michael, I know you like to eat out at restaurants, so you will love this clue. Jesus said that in heaven there is an everlasting banquet. Imagine sitting at a long table with lots of different foods and drinks and every kind of yummy dessert you can think of."

"I hope there will be ice cream sundaes in heaven!" said Abigail.

Grandma laughed. "At this heavenly banquet, people are there from every part of the world—north, south, east, and west. They are talking, laughing, and having a great time. Maybe your grandpa is chatting with someone from a different country and trying some of their favorite foods."

Michael thought a moment and asked, "I wonder who does the dishes in heaven?"

Grandma Nancy walked over to the coffee table and picked up her book of saints.

"The Bible tells us that everyone in heaven is a saint. We don't know all their names, but we do know the names of some of them. Like St. Francis of Assisi, who loved animals. Or St. Patrick, who taught the people of Ireland about God. Or St. Teresa of Calcutta, who cared for poor people.

"The saints did many different things here on earth, but all of them loved Jesus very much and always tried to please him. And because they are so close to God, you can ask them to go to him with whatever you need."

Abigail looked at Grandma Nancy and said, "I wonder if Grandpa has met St. Joseph. That's Grandpa's name, isn't it?"

Grandma said, "Yes, it is. Grandpa and I often prayed to St. Joseph when we needed special help."

Grandma Nancy pulled out her rosary beads. "Here's another clue. Did you know that there's a queen in heaven? It's Mary, the Mother of Jesus! Mary is the most blessed of all women. That's what her cousin Elizabeth said when Mary came to visit her.

"When we pray the fifth glorious mystery of the Rosary, we remember that Mary was crowned queen of heaven. When I pray that mystery, I try to imagine Mary dressed as she's described in the Bible, with the moon under her feet and a crown of twelve stars on her head."

This made Abigail excited. "A queen in heaven! When I see her, I'm going to ask if I can hold her crown."

Grandma nodded and said, "And because Mary is our queen too, we can ask her to go to Jesus with our prayer requests. Jesus loves listening to his mother!"

Grandma Nancy thought for a minute. "Here's a clue about heaven that makes me happy, especially when I'm feeling sad about Grandpa. You and I can't see heaven, but it's really not far away. At every Mass, heaven and earth meet when the bread and wine become Jesus' body and blood. Did you know that angels surround the altar when that happens?"

Abigail smiled and said, "Oh, Grandma, that clue makes me happy too. I'm going to think about heaven when I go to Mass!"

Grandma hugged Abigail and added, "Jesus gave us a great promise, and it's for all of us. He said, 'I am the living bread that came down from heaven; whoever eats this bread will live forever.'"

Michael said, "I'm glad Grandpa was able to be at our First Communion even though he was sick."

"So am I," said Abigail. "I love looking at the photo of him with us on that day."

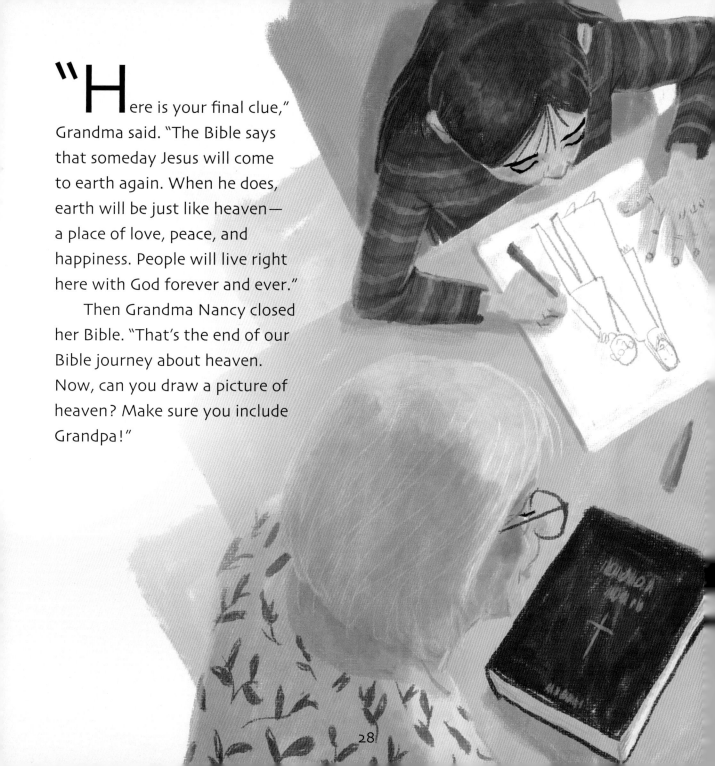

"**H**ere is your final clue," Grandma said. "The Bible says that someday Jesus will come to earth again. When he does, earth will be just like heaven— a place of love, peace, and happiness. People will live right here with God forever and ever."

Then Grandma Nancy closed her Bible. "That's the end of our Bible journey about heaven. Now, can you draw a picture of heaven? Make sure you include Grandpa!"

"That sounds fun!" said Abigail. Michael ran to the drawer in the kitchen where Grandma stored her colored pencils.

"As you begin drawing," said Grandma, "chat with each other about what you think Grandpa is doing right now in heaven."

"I'm going to draw Grandpa playing baseball with his friends," said Michael.

"Abigail thought for a moment and said, "I'll draw Grandpa walking without his cane, next to Jesus on streets of gold!"

Published in 2019 in the U.S. and Canada by
The Word Among Us Press
7115 Guilford Road, Suite 100
Frederick, MD 21704
ISBN: 978-1-59325-358-5

Copyright © 2019 Anno Domini Publishing
www.ad-publishing.com
Text copyright © 2019 Angela M. Burrin
Illustrations copyright © 2018 Gustavo Mazali

Publishing Director: Annette Reynolds
Art Director: Gerald Rogers
Pre-production: Doug Hewitt

Printed and bound in Malaysia

October 2019